Praise for
Building Brownville

Tyler Michael Jacobs' *Building Brownville* is a collection populated by the hard-edged imagery of teeth, knuckles, and "the aroma of vinegar and sick." He writes, "I want you to know the river//From which I come", and the Nebraska landscape is rarely forgiving. Jacobs' landscape is tinted by loss—of a father, of relationships—and yet, these poems are always reaching towards restoration. This is love among the ruins, and Jacobs is a brilliant guide.

-Keith Leonard, author of *Ramshackle Ode*

Tyler Michael Jacobs writes as much about loss as he does love in a place where memories, like Brownville, are recreated and deconstructed. Throughout this journey, you'll browse, mesmerized, through time in lyrical and sensual poems that sing throughout the Great Plains landscape. Whether reminiscing about a lover's body, his father's death, or the prairie's life, the speaker twists and turns in as much a celebration of living as a lamentation of dying. Although at times, Jacobs' world may seem like "the river you love drank itself," this elegant first collection evokes hope for surroundings, "—with the wind in my hair—I'm learning to love." You could say the same of these sinewy poems. As Jacobs rebuilds and breaks down Brownville, he creates a new love for himself throughout Nebraska and beyond that begins with new life.

-Maria Nazos

Tyler Michael Jacob's *Building Brownville* is a collection that shows us the magnificent face of the mundane in "jars of fresh air". A poet of the intimate spaces singing of the mother, of elegy and prayer in a beautifully wrought book of poems. This is a poet rooted in place, capturing the inevitability of life in succinct lines of such lushness and beauty—sometimes tinged with a flowery outburst, most times with vulnerability. Tyler is a poet that listens to the music of things and preserves it for the reader's enjoyment.

-Saddiq Dzukogi, author of *Your Crib, My Qibla*

BUILDING BROWNVILLE

BUILDING BROWNVILLE

poems by
Tyler Michael Jacobs

STEPHEN F. AUSTIN STATE UNIVERSITY PRESS

For more information:
Stephen F. Austin State University Press
P.O. Box 13007 SFA Station
Nacogdoches, Texas 75962
sfapress@sfasu.edu
www.sfasu.edu/sfapress

Managing Editor: Kimberly Verhines
Book design: Katt Noble
Cover design: Katt Noble
Author photo: Kassidy McConville

Distributed by Texas A&M Consortium
www.tamupress.com

ISBN: 978-1-62288-240-3

CONTENTS

❧

For My Father
3 April 1967 to 7 December 2020

And For Nebraska
Both of whom were one and the same.

Bone Teeth

After I prepared for my father to die,
And everything remained uncertain,
I waited—all we can do. Pull love
From the sky in the form of clouds
As the frost on glass thaws
To puddles. I sink into all the blue
Like in the sea. The wind carried
Fever. I stay spit-drunk and cry
About my father's potential of dying
Alone. In the hospital, he eats thanks-
Giving dinner alone—we all eat alone
This year. Buy our groceries for curb-
Side pickup. I want to rip up the roots
Of these plants I bought and feel
As powerful. I want to tell Pete
Ricketts that he is a fucking clown
For the second time. I really just want
For my father to not die. I want to make
These words pretty. I only hope they
Mean something at all. I wish
Into the sink. Nosebleed blooms
And washed out. I spit pieces
Of tooth elsewhere. The taste
Of copper in my mouth. As I speak
With my father, he looks
At the flowers I sent him. Tell me,
I say, can you smell them now?

I

After Don Welch

You walk through the sound
of tall grass
licking

at your legs—to where,
and what, you trace
under your feet:

a memory or the fluttering
of time held
deep in your front shirt

pocket—to write
of familiar places
and those lost in history.

The river you love drank itself
to a chapped bed today:
an hourglass counting

down. You do not believe
the fish would want this.
They rest their fading

heads on pillows
of sand and feel
their bodies burn

to the earth. The fish keep
one eye toward the sky,
forever watching for rain.

Notes On Tomorrow

I pretend to know
who looks

back at me
from the glass.

Dust clings to the air
vent lips exhaling

breath into the room.
We become

familiar with our own
quiet. Each person slips

past another. I drift
over this space.

I'm still realizing
bits of myself I thought

I've long since slept off
like a hangover.

My grandmother
used to drive my cousin

and me around
the block to school

in winter so she could
get out of the house.

We sat in silence
on the backseat.

The key is the breath
in between. I notice

the rose in the vase
hangs its head

as if a child hangs his
too. You believe in me.

I believe we don't have
to speak to get to know

each other. Today
we celebrate the three

clean shirts crumpled
on the floor, tomorrow

we will work
on hanging them

like my uncle,
who left us

to pick the pieces
of his bone

from the yard,
failed to do.

Gunmetal

You grip the stone
of a peach

between
clenched lips.

A light tap
on wood

tops—the redness
on your knuckles.

I trace you.
Your tattoos

on my finger-
tips. All this blue

ink under
my nails from you.

A few soft
thrusts

and what floats
from you:

Truth like a river
never to pass

under a bridge
to look

for light. All else
explodes

from our mouths—
a gasp of color—

and the fuck
of your curve

on sheets.
Little else gushed

as I watched
you eat.

Light Switch

There is the clanging of a bell somewhere
in the darkness. This refines how they teach

us to find God. Imagine what we don't hear:
The cracking of brick in buildings

or lanterns that rip from bellies
and give us unspooled thread

to find a way back into the soft space
of light. Buildings have a way of collecting

people. All loss adds up to something.
As we lie under a mobile of wilted flowers,

we wonder when the gray hair
and the folding of laundry will start.

Nobody should have to clean up the mess
we leave any longer. We listen as the door

creaks open to realize it developed pain—
we were born with it to grow

into ourselves the same way we once grew
into shoes. The day waits as we wait.

This is the sun when there is no more flint
to spark the flame.

What I Heard

As cut grass extends across the lawn

A tree collapses to the crush,

Dust like generations of grief.

A moment in which all moment is lost in the throat.

Unhappiness is not a solitary experience

Like biting a hangnail and bleeding.

As wind brushes across history's face,

We search for something that has never been seen:

Watch water ripple from skipped stones like life

And wonder if you did enough.

If it isn't exposition, you say, then what is the human experience?

On The Farm

The coyotes have yet to be here:
Outside of the fence on a pad
of concrete, a black cow lay dead
and untouched. It was pulled
from the mud and water. The ground
unable to drain wetness for days
which took it early this morning.
If it were to remain here overnight,
the insides would be plucked
and eaten after the singing stops. The cows
follow the fence line snorting at the dirt.
The herd gathers to look at the dead
cow baking in the sun. They look
at their dead the same as we look at ours.

Smudges

There are windows in this city that don't open. I've never seen anything so obviously something be everything that it didn't want to be. *How do those people breathe?* I come home to soggy carpet under the only window in my apartment and imagine God, too, has left windows open in the rain. I write messages on windows throughout this city—like the ones we used to write to each other in the backseat of cars as the world flashed around us. When I rub the fog away now, it is as if I am erasing a part of you.

Threading Carpet

More than a million tiny threads braided together.

You want to become of the other and the other,

this goes on until our hands bleed.

The wind weaves in through the open window that I love

extending itself as I set down a glass of beer.

The aroma of vinegar and sick begins to fill the room,

overtaking lavender and cut grass.

Sometimes it looked like spilt milk.

You cut the tails of the thread to remove the frays

like you snipped the ends of flower stems at an angle,

so the water would drink the jasmine with rose notes,

offering a blush of warmth and I miss that.

The thread becomes an image of the thing that it is not,

darting through one another: A rose or a stalled watch,

perhaps. I was the embellishment of fringe—you were

the square indentation of years.

I remember the quiver of a breast under sheets

and I loved that. I could feel it.

You unfold yourself to me

as the red and white clouds offer themselves

to slats of falling light.

Everything is tangled and glowing

and you weave one last loop into the glass—

drift over the knot.

The thread becomes the thrill of heat. Beside me

a distant whisper as I plummet further into the rug.

Building Brownville

I left their faces bare. Some point, others
Pose and rest fist to hip. More, yet,

Are made to look as if they are hard at work.
Bent, perhaps, at the waist with shovel

Or late, too, for work with briefcase in hand
To wait on a ride that has yet to stop. You sigh.

You asked me to hold bamboo skewers tight
In each fist. Tight enough for you to saw off

The sharp edges to discard. I then cut them
Down further. These will be their fence posts

For a fence line which we leave for the ranch
Hand to finish who forever kneels with hammer

To nail. I imagine he could one day come
To life and realize these posts are held up

By glue. Even the bellowing calf has never made
A sound. These people will find something

In that. It's that hope that makes all this true.
I plotted where their yards will sit, where a boy

Might play with his dog, where a mother might
Shout that dinner is ready from down the street.

After all this, even after we built them homes,
I can't stop thinking about them standing,

Still, expressionless.

II

As From The Mystery

The sky is swollen but the trees still do
Not have leaves to catch the rain.

I imagine that vulnerability to be
Punishment enough. I hear birds aching

Toward life inside soffit and the urgency
Of flutter against metal. And then I kneel

Clench-jawed like all these mice curled
Into themselves on carpeted floors clutch

At their own dying. Somewhere a bereaved
Mother grieves the loss of her son.

Elsewhere, that childhood knots into the earth,
As if the far-off plains were not sweeping

The horizon, now hidden behind cover
Of evergreen and spotty yellow moss.

Further yet, nature rips weathered sheets
To rags on clothesline.

It is the warmth that we don't see:

A little more weight before we create a little
More light.

To Nebraska

You warm me as I curl in your womb.
I must cut myself from where you feed me
like I was cut from where my mother

once fed me. As you hold those I love
to consume in your fertile flesh,
I find comfort in the fact

that you sleep when I sleep. Sometimes
night slips past to float up
from your distant shoulders and leave

us in wonder. Shielding our eyes
from the glisten of light off windowpanes
to look up at the coming blackness

and feel the dust roll in on ourselves.
The grass will bend westward.
We run from what sometimes enters

a room first. I despise your shadow
for betraying me when mine reached out
to say: *You can't lose time, only find it.*

One day I will swallow up your sky and the sun
will fall and keep falling. Until then,
I wake now with my hand over your belly.

Notes On Yesterday

In the dark, we quickly forget how to fall. You learned
Mason jars held light against the cherry tree whose fruit

Filled our stomachs, at which point we realized innocence
Escaped us like the point of night when quiet falls

Too soon. The falling seems as if it never ended. We grew
To stars which fell past the hollow portion of sky as cherry seeds

Scattered the lawn. Water spoiled in the flesh that failed.
I discovered my body alongside

You discovered your body alongside me.
I've never found anything that glowed so brightly before or since.

I've never found anything that glowed so brightly before or since
You discovered your body alongside me.

I discovered my body alongside
Water spoiled in the flesh that failed—scattered the lawn

To stars which fell past the hollow portion of sky as cherry seeds
Grew too soon. The falling seems as if it never ended. We

Escaped us like the point of night when quiet fell
And filled our stomachs. At which point we realized innocence

Held light in Mason jars against the cherry tree whose fruit
Quickly forgot how to fall: In the dark, we learned.

In The Shower

I kneel down to taste you.

Something has spoiled between us. I leave you

to the comfort of the steam and towel myself

dry. You come up on me as I stand at the sink,

lie your face on the nape of my neck.

Your fingers lock together around my waist.

In the moment, we forgive the other's shatter

to the sound of water dotting an empty tub.

The white linoleum under our feet is wet now

as it takes on the sobbing

from the tub floor. You sink into yourself—

raspy breath between the strokes

of my fingers through your wet hair.

Your silhouette against the dull morning

light searches for the part of you not yet finished

off—that flicker of elation you once felt

in your stomach. You would turn in your sleep—

a soft rustling like the cottonwood leaves outside

our bedroom windows. Dropping to the floor

beside me, the thrill of your lips on mine,

I wipe away the leaking to hold you.

She Has Gotten Really Good At Hiding The Fact That She Smokes Cigarettes

i.

There were no stained-glass windows in that Mennonite Church. Instead, the windows carried milky, matte-white glass ignoring how vulnerable she really is. One last time her grandmother set out the spoons and cups before lying down to rest her white curls against the pillow. *Who will pray for us when all of our grandmothers are dead?* she wrote the silent words at the bottom of the funeral programs in ink.

She had never seen anything that used to breathe be everything that it did not want to be.

Think of these windows as our way to share this idea about which we have romanticized when, in fact, we can only make it true in concept and nothing more.

Churches should have, at the very least, opalescent glass in the window frames like the fine china she wasn't allowed to touch as a child. *We award our heirs these sea spray green trinkets to carry from apartment to apartment on their backs to not break a single piece* she thought as she packed it all in boxes.

ii.

She and he moved into a building called The World Apartment Complex. They moved into an apartment where the property manager placed a sign outside The World's gated entryway. They moved into an apartment complex behind a sign which reads: *If you lived here, you'd live in the world.* They lived in The World and grew used to this as a statement of vacancy.

iii.

She watches the clock in her car and remembers
the one that dusted her with snow from heat
vents when she was trying to warm her hands.
She still has to worry about her fear of driving.

iv.

Despite her beauty, she had very ugly knees.

v.

Every morning he wakes and leaves her to sleep an hour longer. He
grabs the green toothbrush from the tumbler glass. Every morning
she wakes and ignores the orange toothbrush in the tumbler glass,
grabbing the green one. Having realized this, they now use gender
specific toothbrushes that make them feel less than one another. They
never tell the other about this feeling.

After a 98-cent composition notebook page full of tally marks
that counted the moments of silence between them, she said:
I want to find somebody so special to bury my ashes on top of.

The last thing she had said to her former lover was through postcard.
It read: *Having a fine time without you.* She signed it simply and with
purpose—She.

vi.

The sound of dead
cell phones and empty school buses
filled her quiet living room
that morning. She stood
watching the news
from the TV set in the corner
and brushed her own growing belly.

Routine's Mornings

I thought habits would come
the way mail does—silently

with time. The sound of rain taps
the window like the black cat that asks

to be let in out of the world.
The house shudders.

I have yet to teach myself
patience and search

the back corners of myself again
just to be sure. I go to the window.

The street glows brackish.
An onset of freeze slows traffic

just a little but it's enough.
I now stand in the water

that drinks yesterday's irks
and catch my reflection

in the pavement
the way anyone catches a cold

in the night. I collect sniffles in sleeves
the way some people save handwriting

to remember what has been lost.
Others run from running noses.

My mind wanders. I think of further habits
that I might have, or never, grew into:

how buildings also have them,
how bones and wood creak similarly

in those early hours.
Maybe habits do the same.

I slide my hand under the pillow
as I slip into bed to relish the cold.

The blue hue of morning rubs
its sleepy eyes awake to watch as I close mine.

Woman Embroidering

You were the brow of a hill

on which a house could have been

built. Always wishing to quit seeing

yourself as the chipped nail polish

that sits on your fingernails. After

the smell of sex inside you

fades into roofless eyes that flow over

the freshly poked green thread,

your luster falters like a sun

washed peach or curtains

without a breeze. You want to draw

a cool bath and open yourself up

to escape the summer rot.

When you die

all of the color fades

from your fingertips.

Your body exhales when it goes

leaving black spots on mattresses

and a glow where you sometimes stood

in the room you loved.

The cat that slept in bed with you

for two years on your back

burying its head in the slope of your neck

loving you with a patience as no man could

is gone. What is left are the remains

of burnt fingertips

from matches used to light the cigarette

of the man you loved held too long.

Harvest

We broke blisters
on our heels
to feed the soil.
Only you didn't
notice. Red faced
as your silver hair
was combed.
I knelt down
to tie your shoe-
laces. A word never
spoken between us.
I wanted to give
you ears
as you tinkered
with time—
your way
of growing older.
I threw pieces
of my bone
from the door-
frame into your
bedroom. Time
passes through
us so quick
that we forget
to think about
the stars and how
they still glow.
I took out another
chunk of my bone.

This one I kept
and left it to rot.
Your bedroom,
an office set
with shelves, full
of silent clocks.
You sat hunched
at your desk
to twist
back seconds
to see—the only
thing in life
that can't be late
is time and you
continue to sweep
the pieces of broken
clock away
from your future
only to stop
and listen
to the hissing
of yourself exhaled.

Nebraska Is Full Of Barren Trees

Three-am rain only lasts long enough
to wake us. I drive south down the striped
state highway toward Loomis—tarred
and rough. The sky is a fogged mirror
too high to clean. Sometimes the wind
is too low for the clouds to move. Pivots
stand idle along barbed wire. Irrigation pipe
lay in white plastic piles in the corner
of plowed and half planted fields. Farmers
park their Chevys at the edge of their crops
to study the soil—debating whether or not
it is too wet to continue to plant corn,
or soybeans. They wait for a while longer
before retreating home for lunch. We turn
our backs to the lavender sky and wait
to greet it like a morning lover. Later, dust
devils violently rip apart nothing. Sometimes
we are that violence against this calm.
All that endures is a heart waiting
to be torn to shreds.

Poking Holes In Butter Dish Lids

In the way back tippy-toe corner of the cupboards
next to the plastic cups—a childhood
version of myself. The empty butter dish containers
that I wash and, without thought, place in those
cupboards above the plates are habits
inherited from my father. In his cupboard,
among the unused bakeware, I find myself
tucked away inside a sealed butter dish
like the ones that line his countertops.

There are remnants of me all over his house—
bookshelves full of outgrown books
about sharks and dinosaurs and insects,
photos taken with disposable cameras
of my brother and me, and dry Wilson leather catching
only spiderwebs. The hole in the plaster
of the kitchen ceiling where I lit off fireworks
is the only memory not found hidden in the dark
corners of the kitchen cupboards and under envelopes
held together by rubber bands that fill the junk drawer.

This year, I tell my brother, *I'm going to learn
to be patient with our father.*
With little left to say, we return to our own lives.

We were young once licking leaves
and sticking them to our skin
as if we could absorb
their powers. We chased our shadows
to the playground where my father explained
all the swear words to me that were written

in black marker on the inside of the spiral tube
slide. I asked if we could call the number
as if we weren't having a good enough time
ourselves. He said: *No. Why?* I asked.
And it was left at that.

Next year, I negotiate with myself,
I'm going to learn what his silence means.
For now, I check the cupboards of every single father
for a glimpse at what they keep
in the way back poking holes in butter dish lids
just to breathe.

III

Building Brownville

I gave them many flowers because they have
Many curtains with nothing to cover

From which they recognize: Pain learns to love
Release. You said to listen, they already know.

Someone will then tell the story of stillness
From under shadow that pads a yard.

The uneven distribution of light in this
Room irks you. A town without trees

Does the same so we gave them trees, too.
You wonder who else will walk these streets.

Maybe there will be a saint, or someone
Who catches many fish. Both as holy

As the last, or the other. Maybe there will be
A daughter who shoulders the weight of her

Bicycle home: A form of prayer. I know
Her parents. I know the feeling that persuades

A hand to a shoulder. And I know these people
Can't lose what can't grow. Yet, they wait

To tell of the moonless sky—A steady harmony
Of hum.

Mise En Place

We are alone together. A breeze intrudes

on this moment from the window

in my kitchen. We welcome this.

You peel off layers of me while you run

everything under hot water first—

cleansing them of rotten freshness

and what is left behind by our hands.

You part everything

into a separate dish and set aside

for later use. Perhaps

this will heal our insides.

We place the makings and mix them together.

We wait.

A cloud of steam divides us. I keep

the question to my lips—

close to me, for now.

You begin to shed articles of clothing

to fight the heat of this room.

To determine if it is done,

we look for the shine that wasn't there before

all of this.

We look at what we made together

and both saw something different.

You woke me early in the morning

when you got up to pee.

I knew you weren't trying

to but we were still spinning

and so stoned that we fell

into each other.

I mistake what is between us:

The question leaking from my lips.

After you leave, your smell stains my sheets.

I hesitate to move out from bed now

knowing that I must wash you from myself.

White Lilies

There are enough cut flowers
on the kitchen counter and table

to make a man. A man is
a shape filled with quiet

and soil-born heft of light.
Shapes are essence:

Distortion like mother's hum
and what is telling of them—

Unending rain
falling from distended bellies

of clouds is a form of love.
If the body is not a mass

of color weighed down by air,
it is then pistiled breath kissing

toward hope. Opening themselves
to scores of rushlight,

these flowers also have shape:
A swelling

against a backdrop of peeled
paint—an act of belief,

or violation. Cloth-like and dainty
hissing up pillars of throats.

A distinction between loss
and birth that helps to pretty a room

with draped windows. To keep
light from spilling forth faces:

In time, all windows open.
These leaves are endlessly in blossom.

Standing Water In Central Nebraska

A dragonfly swarms callow fields;
Paint on a calm, vast canvas.

Duplex

I rise and take five pills by mouth daily.
This I understand. My blood is not good.

      I check again. The blood in me is not good
      Like car oil after three-thousand miles.

Unlike car oil driven on for miles,
My sap will remain my own poison.

      Sap sometimes becomes its own poison
      And leaves pieces of its bone in the hollow.

I'll leave my bones hoping they won't hollow.
The rain weathers everything that we build:

      Whether right or not, we destroy all we build
      To document what the wind tells us is gone.

Saved in documents that tell me I am gone—
I rise and take five pills by mouth daily.

Toadstool

The air chills my leather
spine. As harsh winds blow through

the translucent pages
of myself, I sit on top

of this rock with you. Under light-
less skies, we listen to the echo

of breath sighing
through the long erosion of clay and sand.

After you slipped in the loose dirt,
we share in each other's redness.

It rains a little to remind us
we will fail each other

again. Blades of grass peek
through the cracked earth beneath

our feet. In the slopes of fossil
and stone, souls often get trapped.

Like cicadas buzzing for a mate
in the distant hills,

you rub your thumb across the bony
back of my hand

to the rhythms of the wind
that will one day carry

me as ash through the long grass
of pasture and fence line.

Jars Of Fresh Air

You were spinning the knob
of a phonograph

turntable. The air was cutting
my lips. I crouched down

and felt the electric
veins exposed along the carpet—

how they have remained,
their pulsing—

simple. Everything
in time becomes a light.

When I search the house for you now,
your bedroom hints at a man

I never took the time to know. I regret this.
Jars labeled and put delicately away

on a shelf. I thought
you might have expected this

as you approached the window
to stand in moon-scarred night

collecting fresh air
for when we'll need it most. I then stood

alone; my hands full
of cracked jars. I searched

for a socket to plug your heart back in
and waited, then luminous.

What You Heard

As I drank your mornings starless: A hue the color of breath.

Something like drifting vapor against this curtain

Of birdsongs. Maybe it was the closeness of the horizon

And what I said under it that closed our eyes.

And then it felt quiet at which point there was nowhere to be.

Cloud-like ribbons of shadow blanketed past. Simultaneously

New and ancient like stillness and wind. Understand the muteness

Of rain-washed fingertips at which point I fell in love

With this arterial land. A tree doesn't know how to survive

Without its grief-sounds spilled into air.

Sedimentary

It's quiet inside you as I stand in your heavy
Breath. The wind—your wind—sings for hope.

As you know, a straight line is not
Perfect. Within view, a soft curve of memory

Burning into what you love. Unmoved,
The trees reach out their hands

Toward what they love—the idea of a sky.
I want you to know the river

From which I come. It does not pass through
The way light spills onto a field. It was

Only after that I broke. And with this, I leave you:
The sun sets the way longing fills a chest.

Then I closed my eyes as if they never were before.
Then I closed my eyes, as if they never were before.

Elegy

The trees expose their souls in winter. Purple remains

The hue of death as felled trees rot and drape frosted propane

Tanks. Friction settled in the palm. We never think

Of having to begin again as if the sun drowned and groundhogs

No longer played in the yard. I tell my brother, as we remove

The doors to our father's house, that the air inside these walls

Killed him. He takes deep breaths through his shirt. I

Hack and wheeze with my palms and knees in the sand

Blown yard before sunset. A few more months

And everything will return as if wounds were never opened.

IV

Maple

It was not the exposed roots that bothered me
but what I could not bring

myself to say. And what I could not fashion
for you: A space in me.

An understanding
of all moments I lifted you toward the sky.

We fed squirrels corn and peanuts. My arms
shine with aches. But I lack iron. I've always held

you close. I watched where your steps left me.
This space will always remain

as if it were a punctuated clause
that decorates a dullness. That is

both equal and unequal
to the collapse of clouds.

A memory that all memory fits. I heave.
It feels as if I have been falling my entire life.

In 1999, I Sit At The Kitchen Table And Watch My Father Open Mail Before I Go To Live With My Mother

Take a peek into myself—
the imprecise watch

you keep from winding on your wrist
to tick. Don't leave me alone on this egg-

shell white. Worn by weather
to hold rhythm in the gut.

I prefer a dry room and a surface
on which to sleep like men under

crumples of blankets.
Allow your fists to hold me

to light searching for translucence
to find something. I am no longer

licked inside. Sometimes stop
by to say hello and I'll watch your finger-

nails scrape down my spine—
eyes dart from margin to margin.

You sigh
as I now flatten into neat little piles.

Lebanon, Nebraska

Gone the way of time are the old
patterns to let die. What breaks
this quiet are birdsongs carried
on breath. Eighteen trees stand
isolated on a distant hill outside
of the broken and boarded up
windows of men like the buildings
without signs to hold the tears
of those that will never christen
cheeks. They watch stiff knees
never walk dusty streets—
as families once packed up
their cars to head to where the sun
and the wind look forward
to the future. Before the rust
of years pulls this from maps
and memory, the ghosts that remain
here hold the living close to say hello.

A Portrait Of My Mother

i.

We discovered who we were by writing our names between the lines.
Every night, under the covers with a flashlight, I practiced until there were
        no more lines to write between.
Holding it, arms stretched out, I looked at who I was and it was perfect.

ii.

I presented her my name and watched her trace every indentation
      of my hard work.
She stuck them to the door of the refrigerator which told me she understood.

iii.

When we had to bring a photo of ourselves and paint a self-portrait,
I tucked it inside *Alice in Wonderland* to keep the corners from bending.
My mom said to be careful with it as if it wasn't plucked from a pile of me.
You have to take care of the memories you have she said
Carrying a photo of yourself is like carrying an image of God.

iv.

Mrs. Goldfish explained that running paint lines do not suggest flaws
      within ourselves.
But how do I get the hair just right? I asked.
Maybe you don't.

v.

I would one day paint a portrait of my mother standing in the kitchen
      as she complained of numb fingertips.
Is it all done yet? she asked.
I stood brushing her invisible locks and let the paint lines run so she would know.

Like Prayer

The way to a horse's heart holds
simple. A few slow puffs of breath
into the nostrils, but I learned other ways

to love him. My arms a whisper around
his crest: hands lost in the great sorrel
mane. Clumps of winter shed from his

coat. The wind takes his shimmer
from my hand to abandon it to wilt.
I never wanted to absorb that wind.

The wind I want rips through me
as I rub my hand across his withers
and down his back where a saddle

once sat for years. Inside me,
a shape that resembles the moon.
I place my hand on his muzzle.

We no longer bury the horse with the rider.
He takes the sugar cube from the palm
of my hand to leave each other to the wind.

Something To Get Lost In

Our windowsill now holds the bulbs of cut green onion

to sprout. A sill on which we grow

lemon basil. To wash our hands

with soil from clay pots. I imagined this life.

A life in which we have a window

we both love. This apartment

has so few rooms to decorate.

I cut these flowers under water out of compassion.

We are like moments, color-like and rag-spit

soft, collecting in boxes. These flowers breathe

from the open surfaces

into the room, and snake plant

reaches elegant leaves upward. Each young

and a glimmer of life. We will have to change

the water before planting the green onion

to root: preparing what we destroy

for life. Or a version of it.

You come to me like the wind

pulls our curtains toward fog-cloud. Through the window,

I look out now among the shade-like night

to sunken shadows hefted

across our walls. You are so bright.

So quiet.

Now a glass of water spills over

my bedside table. It was not then, but later,

that I saw you smile at me,

if you ever had before.

How To Sand and Varnish Floodboards

You walk from room to room
to search for blemishes

in the wood. You want
to do this to yourself

as you wear your father's shirt.
Some stains never come out.

You learned this
when you were young

and fell, simply,
through his reach.

You cannot fall from the floor,
only to it.

Your father would wear
this shirt, too,

as he would sand ugliness
from what we walk on.

The smell of varnish
was a sign of home—

at least a symptom
of it. The night stains

your portrait
into the glass

abandoning you
before it's all done with.

The varnish underneath your eyes
remains unfinished

like the floors
your father left for you

uncovered to bask in the moonlight
of this house.

You sand every pockmark and knot
from the floorboards

as easily as turning pages
in the night

before you cut
the shirt to ribbons on the floor.

June 21: Poem for Kearney

There's just enough quiet in the dark streets
to hear the rumble of bicycle rubber

on pavement. Steam impersonates a ballet dancer
in the spotlight of dim streetlamps

at passed through intersections. The small-town streets I ride smell
of hidden imperfections like family secrets gossiped about
            before silent dinners;

and for a moment the quiet subsides as I pass spent condoms,
littered bottles and howls of neglected youth lost to this city

as I sweep under spotlights on 25th Street. The stage void
of encores and the ballerina doesn't take her final bow
            before the applause of rain draws her

from the night. The clicking of my bicycle is again
the only sound in the darkness of three-am
and I look at my city that—with the wind in my hair—
            I'm learning to love.

Catch

The smack of fist in faded
Wilson leather—of my father's

Mitt, where he, too,
Once thwacked fist to paw

To wait as I now wait—echoes
Off the Nebraska sky. My nephew

Greases up the ball with spit.
Like my father

Used to run after my throws over sand
And prickly pear cactus, I chase his

Until the pop of ball to glove
In the prairie grass blows

Us further from the moment. I fall
Back into the boy I was at his age

Watching him
Pause before he—like the ball

In the sun—is blinded into manhood.

I toss the baseball back
Into his mitt to wait again.

Building Brownville

You will paint the skies that lie
behind what breathes—

A door that opens. The ornaments
set aside on a towel to dry. The glue

to hold them to the varnished
popsicle stick clapboard siding

of yesterday. A tooth that hangs
over that opening. All lost

in passing find a door like this.
A hand running along

the face of a river. Brushing on
to what it will leave

and what it will take
with it sealed under resin

for the illusion of movement.
You realize the wind will never

fill or abandon the plastic people
you lower by the hips into place. Shadows

smoke up from synthetic tulips that wait
to open their petals to the florescent sun.

Notes

"Building Brownville": This triptych of poems takes its name from Brownville, Nebraska.

"Catch": After William Kloefkorn's "Out-and-Down Pattern."

"June 21: Poem for Kearney": After Matt Mason's "September 21: Poem for Omaha."

"Maple": "A memory that all memory fits" is my variation of a line from Forrest Gander's "What It Sounds Like" from *Be With* (New Directions Books, 2018).

"Woman Embroidering": The title is taken from the Biedermeier-style painting by Georg Friedrich Kersting c. 1814.

Acknowledgments

I would like to thank the editors of the following journals, who first published versions of these poems:

Aurora: The Allegory Ridge Poetry Anthology: "Notes on Tomorrow"

Burnt Pine Magazine: "To Nebraska"

The Carillon: "After Don Welch"

East by Northeast Literary Magazine: "Threading Carpet"

Funicular Magazine: "Light Switch"

The Good Life Review: "Standing Water in Central Nebraska"

HASH Journal: "Maple"

The Hole in the Head Review: "She has Gotten Really Good at Hiding the Fact That She Smokes Cigarettes"

Labyrinthe: "Routine's Mornings"

LAMP Anthology: "How to Sand and Varnish Floorboards"

The Magazine: "A Portrait of My Mother" and "Poking Holes in Butter Dish Lids"

Open: Journal of Arts & Letters: "Elegy"

Polaris: An Undergraduate Journal of Arts and Literature: "Smudges"

Rumble Fish Quarterly: "Duplex"

Runestone: "June 21: Poem for Kearney"

Second Chance Lit: "Mise en Place"

Thin Air Magazine: "What You Heard"

The Wax Paper: "Notes on Yesterday" and "White Lilies"

White Wall Review: "Bone Teeth" and "Jars of Fresh Air"

The Whorticulturalist: "Gunmetal"

"June 21: Poem for Kearney" was reprinted in *The Carillon*

"Maple" was reprinted in *LAMP Anthology*

TYLER MICHAEL JACOBS was born and raised in central Nebraska. He is a graduate of the University of Nebraska at Kearney and works for the Nebraska Writers Collective as a Teaching Artist. He lives in Kearney, Nebraska.